50 Complete Mushroom Lover's Cookbook Recipes

By: Kelly Johnson

Table of Contents

- Mushroom Risotto
- Creamy Mushroom Soup
- Stuffed Portobello Mushrooms
- Garlic Butter Mushrooms
- Mushroom Stroganoff
- Mushroom and Spinach Frittata
- Wild Mushroom Pasta
- Grilled Mushroom Skewers
- Mushroom Tacos
- Mushroom Quiche
- Sautéed Garlic Mushrooms
- Mushroom and Cheese Stuffed Chicken
- Mushroom Risotto Balls (Arancini)
- Mushroom Bolognese
- Creamy Mushroom and Herb Sauce
- Mushroom and Asparagus Stir-Fry
- Mushroom Pizza
- Balsamic Glazed Mushrooms
- Mushroom and Pea Salad
- Creamy Mushroom Polenta
- Mushroom Pot Pie
- Stuffed Mushrooms with Sausage
- Roasted Mushroom Salad
- Mushroom and Barley Soup
- Thai Mushroom Curry
- Mushroom and Sweet Potato Enchiladas
- Grilled Portobello Burgers
- Mushroom Fried Rice
- Mushroom and Lentil Tacos
- Cheesy Mushroom Casserole
- Mushroom and Broccoli Stir-Fry
- Mushroom Risotto with Peas
- Spinach and Mushroom Stuffed Shells
- Creamy Mushroom Pasta Bake
- Mushroom and Zucchini Gratin

- Mushroom and Cauliflower Tacos
- Mushroom and Feta Stuffed Peppers
- Spicy Mushroom Stir-Fry
- Mushroom and Herb Potato Bake
- Baked Mushroom Falafel
- Mushroom and Bacon Jam
- Miso Mushroom Soup
- Herb and Garlic Roasted Mushrooms
- Mushroom and Ricotta Stuffed Crepes
- Mushroom Ragu
- Mushroom and Chickpea Curry
- Mushroom and Kale Salad
- Stuffed Mushrooms with Goat Cheese
- Mushroom and Quinoa Pilaf
- Smoked Mushroom Dip

Mushroom Risotto

Ingredients:

- 1 cup Arborio rice
- 4 cups vegetable broth
- 1 cup mushrooms, sliced
- 1 onion, diced
- 2 cloves garlic, minced
- 1/2 cup Parmesan cheese, grated
- 2 tablespoons olive oil
- Salt and pepper to taste
- Fresh parsley for garnish

Instructions:

1. **Sauté Aromatics:** In a pot, heat olive oil over medium heat. Add onion and garlic, sauté until soft.
2. **Add Mushrooms:** Stir in mushrooms and cook until browned.
3. **Cook Rice:** Add Arborio rice, stirring for 1-2 minutes. Gradually add vegetable broth, one ladle at a time, stirring until absorbed.
4. **Finish Risotto:** Once rice is creamy and al dente, stir in Parmesan cheese. Season with salt and pepper. Garnish with parsley before serving.

Creamy Mushroom Soup

Ingredients:

- 1 lb mushrooms, chopped
- 1 onion, chopped
- 2 cloves garlic, minced
- 4 cups vegetable broth
- 1 cup heavy cream
- 2 tablespoons olive oil
- Salt and pepper to taste
- Fresh thyme for garnish

Instructions:

1. **Sauté Vegetables:** In a large pot, heat olive oil. Add onion and garlic, sauté until translucent.
2. **Cook Mushrooms:** Stir in chopped mushrooms and cook until softened.
3. **Simmer Soup:** Add vegetable broth and bring to a simmer. Cook for 15 minutes.
4. **Blend and Add Cream:** Use an immersion blender to puree the soup. Stir in heavy cream and season with salt and pepper. Garnish with fresh thyme.

Stuffed Portobello Mushrooms

Ingredients:

- 4 large portobello mushrooms
- 1 cup breadcrumbs
- 1/2 cup Parmesan cheese, grated
- 1/2 cup spinach, chopped
- 2 cloves garlic, minced
- 2 tablespoons olive oil
- Salt and pepper to taste

Instructions:

1. **Preheat Oven:** Preheat oven to 375°F (190°C).
2. **Prepare Filling:** In a bowl, mix breadcrumbs, Parmesan cheese, spinach, garlic, olive oil, salt, and pepper.
3. **Stuff Mushrooms:** Place portobello caps on a baking sheet and fill each with the breadcrumb mixture.
4. **Bake:** Bake for 20-25 minutes until mushrooms are tender and tops are golden.

Garlic Butter Mushrooms

Ingredients:

- 1 lb mushrooms, whole
- 4 tablespoons butter
- 4 cloves garlic, minced
- 2 tablespoons parsley, chopped
- Salt and pepper to taste

Instructions:

1. **Melt Butter:** In a skillet, melt butter over medium heat.
2. **Sauté Mushrooms:** Add whole mushrooms and cook until browned on all sides.
3. **Add Garlic:** Stir in garlic, cooking for another minute. Season with salt and pepper.
4. **Finish:** Remove from heat, sprinkle with parsley before serving.

Mushroom Stroganoff

Ingredients:

- 1 lb mushrooms, sliced
- 1 onion, sliced
- 2 cups vegetable broth
- 1 cup sour cream
- 2 tablespoons flour
- 2 tablespoons olive oil
- 1 tablespoon Worcestershire sauce
- Salt and pepper to taste
- Cooked egg noodles for serving

Instructions:

1. **Sauté Vegetables:** In a skillet, heat olive oil over medium heat. Add onion and mushrooms, cooking until soft.
2. **Add Flour:** Sprinkle flour over the mushroom mixture and stir for 1-2 minutes.
3. **Simmer:** Gradually add vegetable broth and Worcestershire sauce. Simmer until thickened.
4. **Add Sour Cream:** Stir in sour cream and season with salt and pepper. Serve over cooked egg noodles.

Mushroom and Spinach Frittata

Ingredients:

- 1 cup mushrooms, sliced
- 2 cups spinach
- 6 eggs
- 1/2 cup milk
- 1/2 cup cheese, shredded
- 2 tablespoons olive oil
- Salt and pepper to taste

Instructions:

1. **Preheat Oven:** Preheat oven to 350°F (175°C).
2. **Sauté Vegetables:** In an oven-safe skillet, heat olive oil over medium heat. Add mushrooms and spinach, cooking until softened.
3. **Mix Eggs:** In a bowl, whisk together eggs, milk, cheese, salt, and pepper. Pour over the vegetables.
4. **Cook:** Cook on the stovetop for a few minutes, then transfer to the oven. Bake for 15-20 minutes until set.

Wild Mushroom Pasta

Ingredients:

- 8 oz pasta (e.g., fettuccine)
- 1 lb mixed wild mushrooms, sliced
- 2 cloves garlic, minced
- 1/2 cup heavy cream
- 1/4 cup Parmesan cheese, grated
- 2 tablespoons olive oil
- Salt and pepper to taste
- Fresh parsley for garnish

Instructions:

1. **Cook Pasta:** Cook pasta according to package instructions; drain.
2. **Sauté Mushrooms:** In a skillet, heat olive oil. Add mushrooms and garlic, cooking until browned.
3. **Add Cream:** Stir in heavy cream and Parmesan cheese, simmering until thickened. Season with salt and pepper.
4. **Combine:** Toss cooked pasta with the mushroom sauce. Garnish with fresh parsley.

Grilled Mushroom Skewers

Ingredients:

- 1 lb mushrooms, whole
- 2 tablespoons olive oil
- 2 tablespoons balsamic vinegar
- 2 cloves garlic, minced
- Salt and pepper to taste

Instructions:

1. **Marinate Mushrooms:** In a bowl, mix olive oil, balsamic vinegar, garlic, salt, and pepper. Add mushrooms and let marinate for 30 minutes.
2. **Preheat Grill:** Preheat the grill to medium-high heat.
3. **Skewer and Grill:** Thread marinated mushrooms onto skewers. Grill for 5-7 minutes, turning occasionally, until tender and charred.
4. **Serve:** Remove from skewers and serve warm.

Mushroom Tacos

Ingredients:

- 8 small corn or flour tortillas
- 1 lb mushrooms, sliced
- 1 onion, diced
- 2 cloves garlic, minced
- 1 teaspoon cumin
- 1 teaspoon chili powder
- 2 tablespoons olive oil
- Salt and pepper to taste
- Fresh cilantro and lime wedges for serving

Instructions:

1. **Sauté Vegetables:** In a skillet, heat olive oil over medium heat. Add onion and garlic, sautéing until soft.
2. **Cook Mushrooms:** Stir in sliced mushrooms, cumin, chili powder, salt, and pepper. Cook until mushrooms are tender and browned.
3. **Assemble Tacos:** Warm tortillas in a dry skillet. Fill each tortilla with the mushroom mixture. Top with cilantro and serve with lime wedges.

Mushroom Quiche

Ingredients:

- 1 pie crust (store-bought or homemade)
- 1 lb mushrooms, sliced
- 1 onion, chopped
- 4 large eggs
- 1 cup heavy cream
- 1 cup cheese, shredded (e.g., Gruyère or cheddar)
- Salt and pepper to taste
- 2 tablespoons olive oil

Instructions:

1. **Preheat Oven:** Preheat oven to 375°F (190°C).
2. **Sauté Filling:** In a skillet, heat olive oil over medium heat. Add onion and mushrooms, cooking until softened. Season with salt and pepper.
3. **Prepare Custard:** In a bowl, whisk together eggs, heavy cream, salt, and pepper. Stir in the sautéed vegetables and cheese.
4. **Bake:** Pour the mixture into the pie crust. Bake for 35-40 minutes until set and golden. Let cool slightly before slicing.

Sautéed Garlic Mushrooms

Ingredients:

- 1 lb mushrooms, whole or halved
- 4 cloves garlic, minced
- 2 tablespoons butter
- 2 tablespoons olive oil
- Salt and pepper to taste
- Fresh parsley for garnish

Instructions:

1. **Heat Pan:** In a large skillet, heat butter and olive oil over medium heat.
2. **Cook Mushrooms:** Add mushrooms and cook until browned and tender, about 5-7 minutes.
3. **Add Garlic:** Stir in garlic, cooking for another minute. Season with salt and pepper.
4. **Serve:** Garnish with fresh parsley before serving.

Mushroom and Cheese Stuffed Chicken

Ingredients:

- 4 boneless, skinless chicken breasts
- 1 lb mushrooms, finely chopped
- 1 cup cheese, shredded (e.g., mozzarella or Swiss)
- 1/2 cup cream cheese, softened
- 2 cloves garlic, minced
- Salt and pepper to taste
- 2 tablespoons olive oil

Instructions:

1. **Preheat Oven:** Preheat oven to 375°F (190°C).
2. **Sauté Mushrooms:** In a skillet, heat olive oil over medium heat. Add mushrooms and garlic, cooking until soft. Remove from heat and stir in cream cheese and shredded cheese. Season with salt and pepper.
3. **Stuff Chicken:** Cut a pocket in each chicken breast. Fill with the mushroom-cheese mixture. Secure with toothpicks if needed.
4. **Bake:** Place stuffed chicken in a baking dish. Bake for 25-30 minutes until cooked through and juices run clear.

Mushroom Risotto Balls (Arancini)

Ingredients:

- 2 cups cooked risotto (preferably leftover)
- 1 cup mushrooms, finely chopped
- 1/2 cup mozzarella cheese, cubed
- 1/2 cup breadcrumbs
- 1/4 cup flour
- 2 large eggs, beaten
- Oil for frying
- Salt and pepper to taste

Instructions:

1. **Prepare Filling:** In a skillet, sauté chopped mushrooms until softened. Mix with cooked risotto, season with salt and pepper, and let cool.
2. **Form Balls:** Take a small amount of risotto mixture, place a cube of mozzarella in the center, and shape into a ball. Repeat with remaining mixture.
3. **Coat Arancini:** Dip each ball in flour, then in beaten eggs, and finally coat with breadcrumbs.
4. **Fry:** Heat oil in a deep pan. Fry arancini until golden brown. Drain on paper towels before serving.

Mushroom Bolognese

Ingredients:

- 1 lb mushrooms, finely chopped
- 1 onion, diced
- 2 cloves garlic, minced
- 1 carrot, diced
- 1 can (14 oz) crushed tomatoes
- 1 teaspoon dried oregano
- 1 teaspoon basil
- Salt and pepper to taste
- Olive oil for sautéing
- Cooked pasta for serving

Instructions:

1. **Sauté Vegetables:** In a large pot, heat olive oil over medium heat. Add onion, garlic, and carrot, cooking until softened.
2. **Add Mushrooms:** Stir in chopped mushrooms and cook until browned.
3. **Simmer Sauce:** Add crushed tomatoes, oregano, basil, salt, and pepper. Simmer for 20-30 minutes until thickened.
4. **Serve:** Toss with cooked pasta and serve hot.

Creamy Mushroom and Herb Sauce

Ingredients:

- 1 lb mushrooms, sliced
- 1 cup heavy cream
- 2 cloves garlic, minced
- 2 tablespoons butter
- 1 teaspoon fresh thyme or rosemary
- Salt and pepper to taste

Instructions:

1. **Sauté Mushrooms:** In a skillet, melt butter over medium heat. Add mushrooms and garlic, cooking until mushrooms are tender.
2. **Add Cream:** Stir in heavy cream and herbs. Simmer until sauce thickens slightly. Season with salt and pepper.
3. **Serve:** Pour over pasta, chicken, or vegetables.

Mushroom and Asparagus Stir-Fry

Ingredients:

- 1 lb mushrooms, sliced
- 1 bunch asparagus, trimmed and cut into 2-inch pieces
- 2 cloves garlic, minced
- 2 tablespoons soy sauce
- 1 tablespoon sesame oil
- Salt and pepper to taste
- Cooked rice for serving

Instructions:

1. **Heat Pan:** In a large skillet, heat sesame oil over medium-high heat.
2. **Cook Asparagus:** Add asparagus and stir-fry for 2-3 minutes until tender-crisp.
3. **Add Mushrooms:** Stir in sliced mushrooms and garlic, cooking for another 3-4 minutes.
4. **Add Sauce:** Pour in soy sauce, stir well, and cook for an additional minute. Season with salt and pepper. Serve over cooked rice.

Mushroom Pizza

Ingredients:

- 1 pizza crust (store-bought or homemade)
- 1 lb mushrooms, sliced
- 1 cup mozzarella cheese, shredded
- 1/2 cup marinara sauce
- 1 tablespoon olive oil
- 2 cloves garlic, minced
- Fresh basil for garnish
- Salt and pepper to taste

Instructions:

1. **Preheat Oven:** Preheat oven to 475°F (245°C).
2. **Sauté Mushrooms:** In a skillet, heat olive oil over medium heat. Add garlic and sliced mushrooms, cooking until mushrooms are tender. Season with salt and pepper.
3. **Assemble Pizza:** Roll out the pizza crust on a baking sheet. Spread marinara sauce over the crust, then top with sautéed mushrooms and mozzarella cheese.
4. **Bake:** Bake in the preheated oven for 12-15 minutes until the crust is golden and the cheese is bubbly. Garnish with fresh basil before serving.

Balsamic Glazed Mushrooms

Ingredients:

- 1 lb mushrooms, whole or halved
- 1/4 cup balsamic vinegar
- 2 tablespoons olive oil
- 2 cloves garlic, minced
- Salt and pepper to taste
- Fresh parsley for garnish

Instructions:

1. **Preheat Oven:** Preheat oven to 400°F (200°C).
2. **Prepare Mushrooms:** In a bowl, combine mushrooms, olive oil, balsamic vinegar, garlic, salt, and pepper. Toss to coat.
3. **Roast:** Spread mushrooms on a baking sheet in a single layer. Roast for 20-25 minutes, stirring halfway through, until tender and caramelized.
4. **Serve:** Garnish with fresh parsley before serving.

Mushroom and Pea Salad

Ingredients:

- 8 oz mushrooms, sliced
- 1 cup peas (fresh or frozen)
- 1/4 cup red onion, thinly sliced
- 2 tablespoons olive oil
- 1 tablespoon lemon juice
- Salt and pepper to taste
- Fresh herbs (like parsley or mint) for garnish

Instructions:

1. **Sauté Mushrooms:** In a skillet, heat olive oil over medium heat. Add sliced mushrooms and cook until tender. Let cool slightly.
2. **Combine Ingredients:** In a bowl, mix sautéed mushrooms, peas, red onion, lemon juice, salt, and pepper.
3. **Serve:** Garnish with fresh herbs before serving.

Creamy Mushroom Polenta

Ingredients:

- 1 cup polenta (cornmeal)
- 4 cups vegetable broth
- 1 lb mushrooms, sliced
- 1 cup heavy cream
- 2 tablespoons butter
- Salt and pepper to taste
- Fresh thyme for garnish

Instructions:

1. **Cook Polenta:** In a pot, bring vegetable broth to a boil. Gradually whisk in polenta. Cook, stirring frequently, until thickened. Remove from heat and stir in butter, salt, and pepper.
2. **Sauté Mushrooms:** In a skillet, melt butter over medium heat. Add sliced mushrooms and cook until browned. Stir in heavy cream and simmer for a few minutes.
3. **Serve:** Spoon creamy polenta onto plates and top with the mushroom mixture. Garnish with fresh thyme.

Mushroom Pot Pie

Ingredients:

- 1 lb mushrooms, chopped
- 1 onion, diced
- 2 cloves garlic, minced
- 1 cup carrots, diced
- 1 cup frozen peas
- 2 tablespoons flour
- 2 cups vegetable broth
- 1 teaspoon thyme
- 1 pre-made pie crust
- Salt and pepper to taste

Instructions:

1. **Preheat Oven:** Preheat oven to 400°F (200°C).
2. **Sauté Vegetables:** In a skillet, sauté onion and garlic until translucent. Add chopped mushrooms, carrots, and cook until softened.
3. **Make Filling:** Sprinkle flour over the mixture, stirring to combine. Gradually add vegetable broth, stirring until thickened. Add thyme, salt, and pepper, then stir in peas.
4. **Assemble Pie:** Pour filling into a baking dish and cover with the pie crust. Cut slits in the crust to vent.
5. **Bake:** Bake for 25-30 minutes until golden. Let cool slightly before serving.

Stuffed Mushrooms with Sausage

Ingredients:

- 16 large mushrooms, stems removed
- 1 lb Italian sausage, casings removed
- 1 cup breadcrumbs
- 1/2 cup Parmesan cheese, grated
- 2 cloves garlic, minced
- 1 tablespoon parsley, chopped
- Olive oil for drizzling

Instructions:

1. **Preheat Oven:** Preheat oven to 375°F (190°C).
2. **Cook Sausage:** In a skillet, cook sausage over medium heat until browned. Drain excess fat and let cool.
3. **Mix Filling:** In a bowl, combine cooked sausage, breadcrumbs, Parmesan cheese, garlic, and parsley.
4. **Stuff Mushrooms:** Fill each mushroom cap with the sausage mixture. Place on a baking sheet and drizzle with olive oil.
5. **Bake:** Bake for 20-25 minutes until mushrooms are tender. Serve warm.

Roasted Mushroom Salad

Ingredients:

- 1 lb mushrooms, sliced
- 4 cups mixed greens
- 1/4 cup walnuts, toasted
- 1/4 cup feta cheese, crumbled
- 2 tablespoons olive oil
- 1 tablespoon balsamic vinegar
- Salt and pepper to taste

Instructions:

1. **Preheat Oven:** Preheat oven to 400°F (200°C).
2. **Roast Mushrooms:** Toss sliced mushrooms with olive oil, salt, and pepper. Spread on a baking sheet and roast for 15-20 minutes.
3. **Assemble Salad:** In a large bowl, combine mixed greens, roasted mushrooms, toasted walnuts, and feta cheese. Drizzle with balsamic vinegar before serving.

Mushroom and Barley Soup

Ingredients:

- 1 lb mushrooms, sliced
- 1 onion, diced
- 2 carrots, diced
- 2 celery stalks, diced
- 1 cup barley
- 6 cups vegetable broth
- 2 cloves garlic, minced
- 1 teaspoon thyme
- Salt and pepper to taste

Instructions:

1. **Sauté Vegetables:** In a large pot, sauté onion, carrots, and celery until softened. Add garlic and mushrooms, cooking until mushrooms are tender.
2. **Add Broth and Barley:** Stir in vegetable broth, barley, thyme, salt, and pepper. Bring to a boil.
3. **Simmer:** Reduce heat and simmer for 30-40 minutes until barley is cooked. Adjust seasoning as needed before serving.

Thai Mushroom Curry

Ingredients:

- 1 lb mushrooms, sliced
- 1 can coconut milk
- 2 tablespoons red curry paste
- 1 bell pepper, sliced
- 1 onion, diced
- 2 cloves garlic, minced
- 1 tablespoon ginger, grated
- 2 cups spinach
- 2 tablespoons soy sauce
- Fresh cilantro for garnish
- Cooked rice for serving

Instructions:

1. **Sauté Vegetables:** In a large pan, heat a tablespoon of oil over medium heat. Add onion, garlic, and ginger, cooking until fragrant.
2. **Add Mushrooms and Peppers:** Add sliced mushrooms and bell pepper, cooking until tender.
3. **Make Curry:** Stir in red curry paste and coconut milk, bringing to a simmer. Add soy sauce and spinach, cooking until spinach wilts.
4. **Serve:** Garnish with fresh cilantro and serve over cooked rice.

Mushroom and Sweet Potato Enchiladas

Ingredients:

- 1 lb mushrooms, chopped
- 1 medium sweet potato, peeled and diced
- 8 corn tortillas
- 1 can enchilada sauce
- 1 cup cheese (cheddar or Monterey Jack), shredded
- 1 tablespoon olive oil
- 1 teaspoon cumin
- Salt and pepper to taste

Instructions:

1. **Preheat Oven:** Preheat oven to 375°F (190°C).
2. **Cook Sweet Potato:** Boil diced sweet potato until tender, then drain.
3. **Sauté Mushrooms:** In a skillet, heat olive oil, add mushrooms, cumin, salt, and pepper, cooking until mushrooms are browned.
4. **Fill Tortillas:** Mix sweet potatoes with sautéed mushrooms. Fill each tortilla with the mixture, roll them up, and place in a baking dish.
5. **Top with Sauce and Cheese:** Pour enchilada sauce over the rolled tortillas and sprinkle cheese on top. Bake for 20-25 minutes until cheese is melted and bubbly.

Grilled Portobello Burgers

Ingredients:

- 4 large portobello mushrooms, stems removed
- 4 whole wheat burger buns
- 2 tablespoons balsamic vinegar
- 2 tablespoons olive oil
- 1 teaspoon garlic powder
- Salt and pepper to taste
- Lettuce, tomato, and avocado for topping

Instructions:

1. **Marinate Mushrooms:** In a bowl, whisk together balsamic vinegar, olive oil, garlic powder, salt, and pepper. Add mushrooms and let marinate for 15 minutes.
2. **Grill:** Preheat a grill or grill pan. Grill mushrooms for 5-7 minutes on each side until tender.
3. **Assemble Burgers:** Place grilled mushrooms on buns and top with lettuce, tomato, and avocado.

Mushroom Fried Rice

Ingredients:

- 2 cups cooked rice (day-old is best)
- 1 lb mushrooms, sliced
- 2 eggs, beaten
- 1 cup mixed vegetables (carrots, peas, corn)
- 3 tablespoons soy sauce
- 2 tablespoons sesame oil
- 2 green onions, chopped

Instructions:

1. **Sauté Mushrooms:** In a large skillet, heat sesame oil over medium-high heat. Add sliced mushrooms and cook until browned.
2. **Add Veggies:** Stir in mixed vegetables and cook for a few minutes. Push vegetables to the side and add beaten eggs, scrambling until cooked.
3. **Add Rice:** Stir in cooked rice and soy sauce, mixing well until heated through. Garnish with chopped green onions before serving.

Mushroom and Lentil Tacos

Ingredients:

- 1 lb mushrooms, chopped
- 1 can lentils, drained and rinsed
- 1 tablespoon taco seasoning
- 8 taco shells
- 1 avocado, sliced
- Salsa and fresh cilantro for topping

Instructions:

1. **Sauté Mushrooms:** In a skillet, heat oil over medium heat. Add chopped mushrooms and cook until browned.
2. **Add Lentils and Seasoning:** Stir in lentils and taco seasoning, cooking until heated through.
3. **Assemble Tacos:** Fill taco shells with mushroom-lentil mixture and top with avocado, salsa, and cilantro.

Cheesy Mushroom Casserole

Ingredients:

- 1 lb mushrooms, sliced
- 1 cup rice (uncooked)
- 2 cups vegetable broth
- 1 cup cheese (cheddar or mozzarella), shredded
- 1 onion, diced
- 2 cloves garlic, minced
- 1 teaspoon thyme
- Salt and pepper to taste

Instructions:

1. **Preheat Oven:** Preheat oven to 350°F (175°C).
2. **Sauté Vegetables:** In a skillet, sauté onion, garlic, and mushrooms until tender. Season with thyme, salt, and pepper.
3. **Combine Ingredients:** In a large mixing bowl, combine sautéed mushrooms, rice, and vegetable broth.
4. **Transfer to Baking Dish:** Pour mixture into a greased baking dish, cover with cheese, and bake for 30-35 minutes until rice is cooked and cheese is melted.

Mushroom and Broccoli Stir-Fry

Ingredients:

- 1 lb mushrooms, sliced
- 2 cups broccoli florets
- 2 tablespoons soy sauce
- 1 tablespoon sesame oil
- 2 cloves garlic, minced
- 1 teaspoon ginger, grated
- Cooked rice for serving

Instructions:

1. **Sauté Vegetables:** In a large skillet or wok, heat sesame oil over medium-high heat. Add garlic and ginger, cooking until fragrant.
2. **Add Mushrooms and Broccoli:** Stir in sliced mushrooms and broccoli, cooking until tender.
3. **Add Sauce:** Pour in soy sauce and stir to combine. Serve over cooked rice.

Mushroom Risotto with Peas

Ingredients:

- 1 cup Arborio rice
- 1 lb mushrooms, sliced
- 1 onion, diced
- 4 cups vegetable broth (warmed)
- 1 cup peas (fresh or frozen)
- 1/2 cup Parmesan cheese, grated
- 2 tablespoons olive oil
- Salt and pepper to taste

Instructions:

1. **Sauté Onions and Mushrooms:** In a pot, heat olive oil over medium heat. Add onion and cook until translucent. Stir in mushrooms and cook until tender.
2. **Add Rice:** Add Arborio rice, stirring for 1-2 minutes until lightly toasted.
3. **Cook Risotto:** Gradually add warmed vegetable broth, one ladle at a time, stirring frequently until absorbed. Continue until rice is creamy and al dente, about 18-20 minutes.
4. **Finish with Peas and Cheese:** Stir in peas and Parmesan cheese. Season with salt and pepper before serving.

Spinach and Mushroom Stuffed Shells

Ingredients:

- 12 jumbo pasta shells
- 1 cup ricotta cheese
- 1 cup spinach, cooked and chopped
- 1 cup mushrooms, diced
- 1 cup marinara sauce
- 1/2 cup mozzarella cheese, shredded
- 1/4 cup Parmesan cheese, grated
- 1 tablespoon olive oil
- Salt and pepper to taste

Instructions:

1. **Preheat Oven:** Preheat oven to 375°F (190°C).
2. **Cook Shells:** Cook pasta shells according to package instructions. Drain and set aside.
3. **Sauté Mushrooms:** In a skillet, heat olive oil over medium heat. Add diced mushrooms and cook until browned.
4. **Mix Filling:** In a bowl, combine ricotta cheese, cooked spinach, sautéed mushrooms, salt, and pepper.
5. **Stuff Shells:** Fill each pasta shell with the ricotta mixture and place them in a baking dish. Pour marinara sauce over the shells and sprinkle with mozzarella and Parmesan cheese.
6. **Bake:** Cover with foil and bake for 25 minutes. Remove foil and bake for an additional 10 minutes until cheese is bubbly.

Creamy Mushroom Pasta Bake

Ingredients:

- 8 oz pasta (penne or rotini)
- 1 lb mushrooms, sliced
- 2 cups heavy cream
- 1 cup mozzarella cheese, shredded
- 1/2 cup Parmesan cheese, grated
- 2 cloves garlic, minced
- 1 tablespoon olive oil
- Salt and pepper to taste
- Fresh parsley for garnish

Instructions:

1. **Preheat Oven:** Preheat oven to 350°F (175°C).
2. **Cook Pasta:** Cook pasta according to package instructions until al dente. Drain and set aside.
3. **Sauté Mushrooms:** In a skillet, heat olive oil over medium heat. Add garlic and mushrooms, cooking until tender.
4. **Make Sauce:** Stir in heavy cream, salt, and pepper, cooking until slightly thickened. Combine with cooked pasta and half of the mozzarella and Parmesan cheese.
5. **Transfer to Baking Dish:** Pour the mixture into a greased baking dish, topping with remaining cheese.
6. **Bake:** Bake for 25-30 minutes until golden and bubbly. Garnish with fresh parsley before serving.

Mushroom and Zucchini Gratin

Ingredients:

- 2 cups zucchini, sliced
- 2 cups mushrooms, sliced
- 1 cup heavy cream
- 1 cup cheese (Gruyère or cheddar), shredded
- 1/2 cup breadcrumbs
- 2 tablespoons butter
- 1 teaspoon thyme
- Salt and pepper to taste

Instructions:

1. **Preheat Oven:** Preheat oven to 375°F (190°C).
2. **Sauté Vegetables:** In a skillet, melt butter over medium heat. Add zucchini and mushrooms, cooking until soft. Season with thyme, salt, and pepper.
3. **Layer Gratin:** In a baking dish, layer sautéed vegetables. Pour heavy cream over the top and sprinkle with cheese and breadcrumbs.
4. **Bake:** Bake for 30-35 minutes until golden brown and bubbling.

Mushroom and Cauliflower Tacos

Ingredients:

- 1 lb mushrooms, chopped
- 1 head cauliflower, cut into florets
- 8 corn tortillas
- 1 teaspoon taco seasoning
- 1 tablespoon olive oil
- Avocado and salsa for topping
- Fresh cilantro for garnish

Instructions:

1. **Preheat Oven:** Preheat oven to 400°F (200°C).
2. **Roast Cauliflower:** Toss cauliflower florets with olive oil and taco seasoning. Spread on a baking sheet and roast for 20 minutes until tender.
3. **Sauté Mushrooms:** In a skillet, sauté chopped mushrooms until browned.
4. **Assemble Tacos:** Fill tortillas with roasted cauliflower and sautéed mushrooms. Top with avocado, salsa, and cilantro.

Mushroom and Feta Stuffed Peppers

Ingredients:

- 4 bell peppers, halved and seeded
- 1 lb mushrooms, chopped
- 1 cup feta cheese, crumbled
- 1 cup cooked rice or quinoa
- 1 tablespoon olive oil
- 1 teaspoon oregano
- Salt and pepper to taste

Instructions:

1. **Preheat Oven:** Preheat oven to 375°F (190°C).
2. **Sauté Mushrooms:** In a skillet, heat olive oil over medium heat. Add chopped mushrooms, oregano, salt, and pepper, cooking until tender.
3. **Mix Filling:** In a bowl, combine sautéed mushrooms, cooked rice, and feta cheese.
4. **Stuff Peppers:** Fill each pepper half with the mushroom mixture and place in a baking dish.
5. **Bake:** Cover with foil and bake for 30-35 minutes until peppers are tender.

Spicy Mushroom Stir-Fry

Ingredients:

- 1 lb mushrooms, sliced
- 2 cups mixed vegetables (bell peppers, broccoli, snap peas)
- 2 tablespoons soy sauce
- 1 tablespoon sriracha or chili paste
- 2 cloves garlic, minced
- 1 tablespoon sesame oil
- Cooked rice for serving

Instructions:

1. **Heat Oil:** In a large skillet or wok, heat sesame oil over medium-high heat. Add garlic and cook until fragrant.
2. **Add Mushrooms:** Stir in sliced mushrooms and cook until browned.
3. **Add Vegetables:** Add mixed vegetables and stir-fry for 3-4 minutes.
4. **Add Sauce:** Stir in soy sauce and sriracha, cooking until everything is well coated. Serve over cooked rice.

Mushroom and Herb Potato Bake

Ingredients:

- 4 cups potatoes, thinly sliced
- 1 lb mushrooms, sliced
- 1 cup heavy cream
- 1 cup cheese (cheddar or Gruyère), shredded
- 2 cloves garlic, minced
- 1 tablespoon fresh herbs (thyme or rosemary)
- Salt and pepper to taste

Instructions:

1. **Preheat Oven:** Preheat oven to 375°F (190°C).
2. **Sauté Mushrooms:** In a skillet, sauté garlic and mushrooms until tender.
3. **Layer Potatoes:** In a greased baking dish, layer potatoes, sautéed mushrooms, and herbs.
4. **Add Cream and Cheese:** Pour heavy cream over the top and sprinkle with cheese.
5. **Bake:** Bake for 45-50 minutes until potatoes are tender and cheese is golden.

Baked Mushroom Falafel

Ingredients:

- 1 lb mushrooms, chopped
- 1 can chickpeas, drained and rinsed
- 1/2 cup breadcrumbs
- 1/4 cup parsley, chopped
- 2 cloves garlic, minced
- 1 teaspoon cumin
- Salt and pepper to taste

Instructions:

1. **Preheat Oven:** Preheat oven to 375°F (190°C).
2. **Blend Ingredients:** In a food processor, combine mushrooms, chickpeas, breadcrumbs, parsley, garlic, cumin, salt, and pepper. Blend until mixed but still chunky.
3. **Form Balls:** Shape mixture into small balls and place on a baking sheet.
4. **Bake:** Bake for 25-30 minutes until golden and firm, turning halfway through.

Mushroom and Bacon Jam

Ingredients:

- 1 lb mushrooms, finely chopped
- 4 oz bacon, diced
- 1 onion, finely chopped
- 2 cloves garlic, minced
- 1 tablespoon balsamic vinegar
- 1 tablespoon brown sugar
- Salt and pepper to taste
- Fresh thyme for garnish

Instructions:

1. **Cook Bacon:** In a skillet, cook diced bacon over medium heat until crispy. Remove and set aside, leaving fat in the skillet.
2. **Sauté Vegetables:** Add onion and garlic to the skillet, cooking until soft. Stir in mushrooms and cook until all moisture is evaporated.
3. **Add Flavorings:** Add balsamic vinegar, brown sugar, cooked bacon, salt, and pepper. Cook for an additional 5-10 minutes until jammy.
4. **Serve:** Garnish with fresh thyme and serve on toasted bread or as a condiment.

Miso Mushroom Soup

Ingredients:

- 8 oz mushrooms, sliced
- 4 cups vegetable broth
- 2 tablespoons miso paste
- 2 green onions, chopped
- 1 tablespoon soy sauce
- 1 tablespoon sesame oil
- Seaweed for garnish (optional)

Instructions:

1. **Sauté Mushrooms:** In a pot, heat sesame oil over medium heat. Add mushrooms and cook until soft.
2. **Add Broth:** Pour in vegetable broth and bring to a simmer. Cook for 10 minutes.
3. **Mix Miso:** In a small bowl, mix miso paste with a bit of warm broth until smooth. Stir into the soup.
4. **Season and Serve:** Add soy sauce and green onions. Serve hot, garnished with seaweed if desired.

Herb and Garlic Roasted Mushrooms

Ingredients:

- 1 lb mushrooms, whole
- 4 cloves garlic, minced
- 3 tablespoons olive oil
- 1 tablespoon fresh herbs (thyme, rosemary, or parsley)
- Salt and pepper to taste

Instructions:

1. **Preheat Oven:** Preheat oven to 400°F (200°C).
2. **Prepare Mushrooms:** In a bowl, toss mushrooms with olive oil, garlic, herbs, salt, and pepper.
3. **Roast:** Spread mushrooms on a baking sheet in a single layer. Roast for 20-25 minutes until golden and tender.
4. **Serve:** Serve warm as a side dish or appetizer.

Mushroom and Ricotta Stuffed Crepes

Ingredients:

- 2 cups crepe batter (made with flour, eggs, milk)
- 1 lb mushrooms, sliced
- 1 cup ricotta cheese
- 1/2 cup Parmesan cheese, grated
- 2 cloves garlic, minced
- 1 tablespoon olive oil
- Salt and pepper to taste

Instructions:

1. **Make Crepes:** Prepare crepes according to your favorite recipe or package instructions. Set aside.
2. **Sauté Mushrooms:** In a skillet, heat olive oil over medium heat. Add garlic and mushrooms, cooking until tender. Season with salt and pepper.
3. **Mix Filling:** In a bowl, combine ricotta cheese, sautéed mushrooms, and half of the Parmesan cheese.
4. **Fill Crepes:** Place a spoonful of filling in each crepe and fold.
5. **Bake:** Arrange in a baking dish, sprinkle with remaining Parmesan, and bake at 350°F (175°C) for 15 minutes.

Mushroom Ragu

Ingredients:

- 1 lb mushrooms, chopped
- 1 onion, finely chopped
- 2 cloves garlic, minced
- 1 carrot, diced
- 1 can (14 oz) crushed tomatoes
- 1 teaspoon Italian seasoning
- Olive oil for cooking
- Salt and pepper to taste
- Fresh basil for garnish

Instructions:

1. **Sauté Vegetables:** In a pot, heat olive oil over medium heat. Add onion, garlic, and carrot, cooking until softened.
2. **Add Mushrooms:** Stir in chopped mushrooms and cook until browned.
3. **Add Tomatoes and Seasoning:** Add crushed tomatoes, Italian seasoning, salt, and pepper. Simmer for 20-25 minutes until thickened.
4. **Serve:** Garnish with fresh basil and serve over pasta or polenta.

Mushroom and Chickpea Curry

Ingredients:

- 1 lb mushrooms, sliced
- 1 can (15 oz) chickpeas, drained and rinsed
- 1 onion, chopped
- 2 cloves garlic, minced
- 1 tablespoon curry powder
- 1 can (14 oz) coconut milk
- 2 tablespoons olive oil
- Salt and pepper to taste
- Fresh cilantro for garnish

Instructions:

1. **Sauté Onion and Garlic:** In a pot, heat olive oil over medium heat. Add onion and garlic, cooking until softened.
2. **Add Mushrooms:** Stir in sliced mushrooms and cook until tender.
3. **Add Chickpeas and Curry Powder:** Add chickpeas, curry powder, salt, and pepper. Stir to combine.
4. **Add Coconut Milk:** Pour in coconut milk and simmer for 15-20 minutes.
5. **Serve:** Garnish with fresh cilantro and serve with rice.

Mushroom and Kale Salad

Ingredients:

- 8 oz mushrooms, sliced
- 4 cups kale, chopped
- 1/4 cup olive oil
- 2 tablespoons lemon juice
- Salt and pepper to taste
- 1/4 cup walnuts, toasted
- 1/4 cup feta cheese, crumbled (optional)

Instructions:

1. **Sauté Mushrooms:** In a skillet, heat olive oil over medium heat. Add mushrooms and cook until browned. Set aside to cool.
2. **Prepare Dressing:** In a bowl, whisk together olive oil, lemon juice, salt, and pepper.
3. **Toss Salad:** In a large bowl, combine kale, sautéed mushrooms, walnuts, and feta (if using). Drizzle with dressing and toss to combine.
4. **Serve:** Serve immediately as a fresh side salad.

Stuffed Mushrooms with Goat Cheese

Ingredients:

- 12 large mushroom caps
- 4 oz goat cheese, softened
- 1/4 cup breadcrumbs
- 2 cloves garlic, minced
- 2 tablespoons fresh herbs (parsley, thyme, or chives)
- Salt and pepper to taste
- Olive oil for drizzling

Instructions:

1. **Preheat Oven:** Preheat oven to 375°F (190°C).
2. **Prepare Filling:** In a bowl, mix goat cheese, breadcrumbs, garlic, herbs, salt, and pepper until combined.
3. **Stuff Mushrooms:** Fill each mushroom cap with the goat cheese mixture and place on a baking sheet.
4. **Drizzle with Oil:** Drizzle lightly with olive oil.
5. **Bake:** Bake for 20-25 minutes until mushrooms are tender and filling is golden.

Mushroom and Quinoa Pilaf

Ingredients:

- 1 cup quinoa, rinsed
- 2 cups vegetable broth
- 8 oz mushrooms, sliced
- 1 onion, chopped
- 2 cloves garlic, minced
- 2 tablespoons olive oil
- 1 teaspoon thyme
- Salt and pepper to taste
- Fresh parsley for garnish

Instructions:

1. **Sauté Vegetables:** In a large skillet, heat olive oil over medium heat. Add onion and garlic, cooking until soft. Stir in sliced mushrooms and cook until browned.
2. **Cook Quinoa:** Add rinsed quinoa and vegetable broth to the skillet. Stir in thyme, salt, and pepper. Bring to a boil, then reduce heat to low, cover, and simmer for 15 minutes or until quinoa is cooked and liquid is absorbed.
3. **Fluff and Serve:** Remove from heat, fluff with a fork, and garnish with fresh parsley. Serve warm as a side dish or main course.

Smoked Mushroom Dip

Ingredients:

- 8 oz mushrooms, chopped
- 1/2 cup cream cheese, softened
- 1/2 cup sour cream
- 1 tablespoon smoked paprika
- 2 cloves garlic, minced
- Salt and pepper to taste
- Fresh chives for garnish

Instructions:

1. **Sauté Mushrooms:** In a skillet, heat a little olive oil over medium heat. Add chopped mushrooms and garlic, cooking until mushrooms are browned and liquid is evaporated. Let cool slightly.
2. **Mix Ingredients:** In a bowl, combine cream cheese, sour cream, smoked paprika, salt, and pepper. Stir in the cooled mushrooms.
3. **Chill and Serve:** Refrigerate for at least 30 minutes to allow flavors to meld. Garnish with fresh chives before serving with crackers or veggies.

www.ingramcontent.com/pod-product-compliance
Lightning Source LLC
LaVergne TN
LVHW081334060526
838201LV00055B/2629